I'm Exhausted

What to Do When You're
Always Tired

David Powlison

New
Growth
Press
www.newgrowthpress.com

All Scripture quotations, unless otherwise indicated, are taken from the *Holy Bible,* New International Version®, NIV®. Copyright © 1973, 1978, 1984 by International Bible Society. Used by permission of Zondervan. All rights reserved.

New Growth Press, Greensboro, NC 27404
Copyright © 2010 by Christian Counseling & Educational Foundation
All rights reserved. Published 2010.

Cover Design: Tandem Creative, Tom Temple, tandemcreative.net
Typesetting: Robin Black, www.blackbirdcreative.biz

ISBN-10: 1-935273-72-8
ISBN-13: 978-1-935273-72-1

Library of Congress Cataloging-in-Publication Data

Powlison, David, 1949-
   I'm exhausted : what to do when you're always tired / David Powlison.
      p. cm.
   Includes bibliographical references.
   ISBN-13: 978-1-935273-72-1 (alk. paper)
   ISBN-10: 1-935273-72-8 (alk. paper)
   1. Chronic fatigue syndrome—Patients—Religious life.
I. Title.
   BV4910.335.P69 2010
   248.8′61960478—dc22

                                        2010023095

Printed in Canada
20 19 18 17 16 15 14 13   8 9 10 11 12

If you're reading this minibook, it's likely that you or someone you love is struggling with profound, long-lasting fatigue. After open heart surgery, I experienced shattering and debilitating fatigue for five years. I said to my wife many months after surgery, "I feel like someone who took his car in for repairs. The car I got back turned out to be a junker." The wounds had healed, but my body didn't work.

Fatigue destroyed much of my life. I had no resilience. I was able to do only the bare minimum in every area of my life. I had to let go of many things that were valuable, gratifying, and joyous. My social circle became smaller and smaller, finally narrowing down to family and a few friends. My ministry life—counseling and teaching—was severely curtailed. You've probably experienced similar losses in your struggle with fatigue.

Although I lost much of my social connectedness and ministry, God's ministry to me and his social life with me became incalculably precious and sweet. Because of my deep need for God, my relationship with him became more intimate. Psalm 46 assured me, "God is an ever-present help in trouble." The essential dynamic of my moments and days became, "Lord, this *is* trouble. Help!" And he helped.

God will also help you. Extreme fatigue strips life down to the bare basics of human need and God's grace. As you learn to call upon God, you will find him. He will meet you, sustain you, comfort you, and give you hope. God "comforts us in all our troubles, so that we can comfort those in any trouble with the comfort we ourselves have received from God" (2 Corinthians 1:4). God comforted me in my affliction. This small book is one way God has given me to offer that same comfort to you. I want to share with you the things that God has taught me through one of the hardest times in my life.

Perhaps you are too weary to read this in one sitting. Take a few days. Read one section at a time. As you read, ask God to give you his perspective on your battle with fatigue. Ask him to meet you.

Causes for Debilitating Fatigue

Some people are diagnosed with Chronic Fatigue Syndrome or depression,[1] but those are only two of the possible causes of fatigue. What are the reasons why you might be struggling with fatigue?

- **Physical Problems:** allergies, arthritis, chronic fatigue syndrome, cancer, hypoglycemia,

fibromyalgia, multiple sclerosis, thyroid dysfunction, and many other diseases, medication side effects, sleep problems, old age, and parenting young children (nursing and hormonal changes for women, and loss of sleep for both women and men)
- **Life Stresses:** grief, overwork, broken relationships, difficult circumstances, and a traumatic event
- **Spiritual Struggles:** fear, guilt, worry, hopelessness, and bitterness

Learning to Live with Fatigue

This list of reasons is long, but it's not comprehensive. The reason for your fatigue might not be listed here. You may never find out exactly why you're so tired. Many people don't. In my situation, I faced five years of mystery, with no explanations. Finally, we found both an explanation and a cure. Perhaps you also will find a cause and a cure, but for now you have to learn to live well within fatigue's limitations. You will have to learn how to think, feel, choose, believe, love—and not sin—while you feel like a "dimly burning wick." You need to know God and live fruitfully despite your constant weariness. Is this possible? Yes it is. I know that God used my fatigue, difficult as it was, for good in my life. He plans to do the same for you.

How Our World Sees Fatigue

Start by swimming upstream against our world's perspective on fatigue. How does our world view fatigue?

- *Our world despises fatigue.* It hates weakness, dependency, aging, inability, and weariness. Our culture's ideal is to be strong, independent, youthful, vigorous, capable, radiant, healthy, and energetic. That is a half-truth. To enjoy health and strength *is* a wonderful gift from God. To lose these things is hard. But our culture takes those good gifts and says, "You gotta have them!" And if you don't have them, you are defective. You are less than a human being. The world takes the gifts of God without God. It lives for the gifts, not for the Giver. But God says that weakness is the door to knowing him.
- *Our world treats fatigue only as a medical problem.* We love to give problems a name and try to fix them with a pill or program. Sometimes a

medical diagnosis and treatment can help you. But weakness and fatigue are normal within a fallen world. Our world ignores that reality and abnormalizes the normal by creating or seeking a medical label for something that is ultimately a profound aspect of the human condition.

How God Views Fatigue

God views your fatigue differently. He uses fatigue to teach you important truths. What are those truths?

- *God is in control.* You live in God's world. He made all things and is in charge of everything that happens. Your long-lasting fatigue is not a bad accident. It's under God's control and will be used by him to deepen your relationship with him and to grow you to be more like him. Jesus learned obedience on the long road of weakness and suffering (Hebrews 5:7–8). He will deal gently and sympathetically with you as he makes you like himself (Hebrews 4:14–16; 5:2).
- *You are fundamentally weak and dependent.* When Paul says that "the Spirit helps us in our

weakness" (Romans 8:26), he's talking about what it means to be a creature. We are dust. We are clay. We don't have life in ourselves. We are mortal. And that means we are fundamentally fragile and dependent. Long-lasting, debilitating fatigue is one of the many ways we experience weakness and dependence. Your weakness, tiredness, and fatigue are highlighting what has always been true: you are completely dependent on God for every breath. He makes us know our vulnerability so that we will know our need for him.

Your Fatigue Is a Door to Knowing God

God will use your fatigue as the door into a deeper knowledge of his love. As you read the Psalms, you see that those who know God well know themselves to be afflicted, weak, oppressed, broken, humble, and needy. Psalm 31:5—"Into your hands I commit my spirit"—was on Jesus' lips as he hung on the cross, powerless and in great pain. He became this for us.

Hebrews 4:15 says, "We do not have a high priest who is unable to sympathize with our weaknesses, but we have one who has been tempted in every way, just as we are—yet was without sin." Jesus lived in weakness. He knows what it's like to depend on the mercies of God for every breath. Jesus' experience of weakness is the door to one of the most marvelous promises of God in the next verse: "Let us then approach the throne of grace with confidence, so that we may receive mercy and find grace to help us in our time of need" (Hebrews 4:16).

What is fatigue? It's a very specific time of need. You are struggling. Life is hard. You are living through a dark time. You're living in a body that doesn't work. You need. Your Lord sympathizes with your need. He promises you grace and mercy—immediate help in the context of your need.

Fatigue Helps You to See Your Heart's True Condition

Like any trouble, fatigue exposes what's really going on in your heart and mind. In your trouble you can turn to God for help, or you can turn away from God. Fatigue is a particular kind of trouble that brings its own particular temptations. Here are some ways that you might be tempted to turn from God as you live with fatigue:

1. *Anxiety.* You have lost your health. It's tempting to fret, obsess, and worry about your health, your future, and your identity.

2. *Compulsively seek a cure.* Another typical temptation is to obsess about your health in such a way that it takes over your whole life. Hear me rightly: I am not making light of the goodness of medical care. Certainly you should look for possible help from your doctors. But when you aren't healthy, it's easy to make getting healthy the center of your life.

3. *Escapism.* Because you don't feel like doing anything, it's tempting to just vegetate—turning to food, to television, or to other escapes. Because you feel lousy, it's tempting to find something that will help you forget how you feel.

4. *Use it for secondary gains.* Fatigue gives you a very convenient excuse to not do things. So it's tempting to use it as an excuse to not do even things you are still able to do.

5. *Grumble.* Fatigue will sorely tempt you to grumble. The Israelites did not grumble when they were in

the land of milk and honey. They grumbled when it was hard, when it was hot. They grumbled when they were tired, hungry, and thirsty.

6. *Give up.* To lose so many capabilities, and to have so many things you would like to do but can't is depressing. It's a loss. The temptation to give up in your situation is huge.

7. *Denial.* Maybe you don't give up; instead, you deny you have a problem. You keep going forward, pushing yourself, and trying to do it all. You don't want to admit you have any limitations. You're afraid that if you ever stopped or slowed down you would lose your identity.

8. *Self-pity.* It's tempting to feel sorry for yourself and imagine that your situation is harder than what others face. Comparing hardships is a no-win game.

Can you find your temptations on this list? Perhaps you could add a few more. Think about what underlies your temptations. What is going on in your heart as you struggle with anxiety, discouragement, and escapism?

Perhaps you have found your identity in what you do. Now "doing" is taken away from you. You don't know who you are or what your place is in this world. So you're tempted to despair, to obsess about how to recover your abilities, or to try to escape the new reality of your life.

Or perhaps you notice that behind your escapism and irritation is a demand for certain things that you want from life: "I want _____. I fear its opposite." The Bible calls these demands "desires of the sinful nature" (Galatians 5:16; Ephesians 2:3; 1 John 2:16). Desires or cravings of the sinful nature are not just sexual or financial. They're anything you want more than the living God. These are your god-substitutes. For instance, "I want my social life. I fear being isolated. I need entertainment. I just want to feel better." There's nothing wrong with enjoying friends and family–but when your fatigue takes good things away, your response will show you if you were making them the center of your life. Your fear and obsession are pointing to what you worship instead of God.

There is only one thing to do when you feel trapped by your response to fatigue. You turn. You turn away from your false identity and false desires toward the living God. Turn to him in repentance and ask for mercy. Turn to God every day and every moment. Turn to Jesus who sympathizes with your weakness. He has experienced your temptations, and he promises to help you in your time of need. This is what the life of faith is all about—noticing your sins and relying on Jesus for forgiveness and help. His death and resurrection guarantee that you will be forgiven and helped. They guarantee that one day your tears will be wiped away and you will be with God, strong and healthy forever (Revelation 21:3–4).

Your Fatigue Reveals God's Power

As you turn to God, he will help you by changing the way you think about your life. Instead of despising your weakness, you will see that your weakness reveals God's power. Pour out your heart to God just like Paul did in 2 Corinthians 12. He had a weakness that he called a "thorn in my flesh." He begged God to take his weakness away. He said, "Three times I pleaded with the Lord to take it away from me" (vv. 7–8).

Paul received from God this response: "My grace is sufficient for you, for power is made perfect in weakness" (v. 9, author paraphrase). God's power is perfectly revealed in our weakness. God will use your weakness to show you that what drives your life is not you, but the power and mercy of Another.

Paul responded to God by saying, "I will boast all the more gladly about my weaknesses, so that Christ's power may rest on me" (v. 9). The very things that the world despises become the occasions for the power of Christ to be displayed in Paul's life. Then Paul said, "For Christ's sake, I delight in weaknesses, in insults, in hardships, in persecutions, in difficulties" (v. 10). Such troubles are no fun to experience. But he's content in them for Christ's sake, and he concludes, "For when I am weak, then I am strong" (v. 10). That even sounds un-American! People value being strong and independent. But the dynamic of weakness and dependency makes Christ matter in your life. When Christ matters in your life, he shines through your life. People see the evidence of something wonderful—the hand of Another at work in you.

God's Character Shines through Your Weakness

When others look at you, they will see the evidence of God's divine power at work in you. You are doing things, thinking things, processing things, accepting things in a way that "normal" human beings with typical fears, obsessions, and compulsions don't.

You can see this in Paul. He lives life in a radically different way. He sees that his suffering—his thorn in the flesh—serves a good purpose. God is using it to keep him humble, to protect him from exalting himself. When you turn to God in your weakness, things start to happen that you would have once thought were impossible—things such as learning deep contentment and living with a profound sense of purpose. You will speak of your weakness as the place God most richly reveals himself to you.

Fatigue forces you to wrestle with how your life still counts even when what you do, how much you do, and how often you can do it are greatly reduced. God is more interested in who you are in Christ than in what you do for him. God wants you to grow to be like him. He wants your character to resemble his character. Your fatigue is the context he is using to make his character shine through your life.

God wants to use your fatigue to teach you his patience, endurance, perseverance, and longsuffering (Romans 12:12; 1 Corinthians 13:4; Ephesians 4:2).

As you turn from the temptations that come with fatigue and accept your limitations, God will be teaching you the patient purposefulness of Christ himself.

Practical Strategies for Change

How does the way you live change as you take to heart these truths about your weakness and God's power? How do you actually live within the limitations of fatigue? We have already talked about facing your weakness with faith. And faith always expresses itself in love. But how can you love those around you when you have no energy? Here are some things you can do, even within the limitations of your fatigue.

Depend on Jesus One Day at a Time

Yes, this can be misused and turned into a truism. But it happens to be true. Jesus says, "Therefore do not worry about tomorrow, for tomorrow will worry about itself. Each day has enough trouble of its own" (Matthew 6:34). Jesus wants you to depend on him one day at a time. Learn not to worry about tomorrow. You could be cured tomorrow. You could be cured only when you see the

Lord face-to-face. But whatever your future, you are called to live by faith today.

To do this you must meditate on who Jesus is. More than any other passage, Psalm 23 brought Jesus to life for me in my struggles with fatigue. The psalm is full of promises—he provides, he restores my soul, he is with me, his goodness and mercy pursue me all of my days. Make this psalm your own. Jesus, your good Shepherd, will fill you with confidence. God doesn't meet us the way we want, but he does restore us. No matter what you are facing, you have a Shepherd who is with you, restoring you, and bringing good things—himself—into your life. Learn to trust him, and you truly have something worth living and dying for.

Think Small

One of the keys to living with fatigue is to scale down the size of your life. Think about everything in your life in terms of two nesting circles—one large and one small. Put in the big circle all the ideals you would like to become reality—your children grown and perfect, your health restored, your life trouble free. Then put in the smaller circle only those things you are actually responsible for. What are you called to do in this world? When you have debilitating fatigue that inner circle gets small. There's much less you can do and much less you are called to do.

We live in a "Go, go, go!" culture that values achievement and productivity. It doesn't value restorative or recuperative times unless it's a get-away vacation that recharges your batteries so you can get back to the rat race. But what if you can't get back to the rat race? What will be the quality of your days if you are slowed by fatigue? There is a holy rhythm of rest and work. That rhythm may be very different at one stage of your life from another. But at every stage you are called to live for God, not the god of productivity. He wants to teach you how to live for him through small obediences. Little things can show your love for God and others.

Instead of spending your time thinking about what you can't do, ask yourself, "What can I do?" Perhaps it's something as small as saying "thank you," remembering a person's name. It might be as simple as brushing your teeth, emptying the trash, picking up a sock from the floor. It might mean greeting your family warmly, or praying for a struggler. Take a quiet walk and *notice*—sun, tree, cloud, people. It surely means *not* to grumble and complain. That's not small; it's big.

There are good things you are not too tired to do—maybe not a lot, but there are always some. God is calling you to the obedience of faith that leads to the obedience of love. These "small obediences" show up in small acts of kindness and care that will make your life sparkle.

Pursue Medical Help without Obsessing

Look for help from medicine, but don't make that the center of your life. There is no formula for this. It will be different for different people. You need to develop wisdom in this area of your life so you know when you are putting too many of your eggs in a medical cure basket. Our culture is often of little help, because it is obsessed with health. The people who love you and care for you will often want to talk a lot about medical issues. You need to learn how to graciously change the subject to the more important things God is teaching you. You should seek appropriate medical help while still living your life within the circumstances God has given you.

Help Others Deal with Your Fatigue

You can show your love to your family and friends by helping them deal with your fatigue. First, recognize that your fatigue also creates suffering for those around you. During my five-year struggle with fatigue, I got all the attention. But my wife Nan suffered as much as I did. She had to function like a single person in much of her social relations. She had to deal with a husband whose energies were very unpredictable. Some days I was almost normal; other days I was barely functional.

Second, as you notice that your fatigue causes others to suffer, you can love them by doing something as small as asking, "How are you doing?" Remember, their experience and what God is doing in them is just as important as what he is doing in you. Your fatigue is not only about you. God is using suffering to weave your lives together. And, even though you are weak, he is calling you to love those who are suffering along with you.

Third, graciously listen to all the advice you get, but don't feel like you have to follow all of it. If I had taken every bit of advice I received over the years, I would be on eighty-three contradictory diets and spending hundreds of dollars every week on vitamin supplements! The advice others give you is well-meaning—nobody wants to hurt you. They want to help you. But we live in a "fix-it" culture, and your friends and relatives will often try to fix you. There might even be people who criticize you because you didn't go on that diet, or see that doctor, or do the same thing that helped their third cousin once removed. Others might view your fatigue as purely a spiritual issue, and they will tell you that if you had more faith or trust in God you would be healed. That is both false and harmful. Many people learn to trust in the context of *not* being healed. Sometimes you will have to forgive those who love and care about you.

Fourth, share with them how God is helping you to live in his world within the limitations of your fatigue, and how God is using your fatigue to make you more like him. There are many ways you can bear witness to the ongoing work of God in your life in areas other than physical healing. For example, God has helped me to write articles on the Psalms over the last few years. I never could have written these articles when I felt fine. Without going through the difficulties of shattering fatigue, I would not have been able to deeply appreciate the struggles of others who were also going through hard things. Without suffering with fatigue, I wouldn't be able to understand the parts of the Bible that are about hard things. I am delighted that God has strengthened me physically, but growth in faith and love that God has worked in me is the weightier blessing. You will bless the people around you if you help them to see this. Hearing from you what God is doing in your life will free them from their anxiety about you and help them to live better in God's world.

A Personal Note

In the spring of 2006, God cured me of my fatigue. My doctors realized that cardiac medicines and an inability to get a restful night's sleep were the cause of my fatigue. We changed a few simple things and much of my energy and resilience was restored.

The answer to my fatigue turned out to be so simple. Why did no one ever carefully inquire during those five long years? Why did it take so long to find out why I couldn't function? I can't answer those questions, but I do know that my experience with fatigue drew me deeper into intimacy with God and prepared me to love others by offering the comfort that I have received. These thoughts on living by faith with fatigue were forged in the furnace of my own life and the mercies of God for me. Not one second of the dreariness and difficulty of those five years has been wasted, except for what I wasted when I lost sight of God.

Although you are living with severe limitations right now, your life is not a waste. God heard my cry for help and met me. He will do the same for you. He will pour his wisdom and kindness into your heart as you cry out to him. Then whether your physical restoration comes in this life or at your resurrection from the dead, you will see that you have the one indestructible thing in this world: the Lord *is* your Shepherd and his goodness and mercy will follow you all the days of your life.

Endnotes

1 For a very helpful book on depression see Edward T. Welch, *Depression: A Stubborn Darkness* (Greensboro, NC: Punch Press, 2004).